# God's Little Instruction Book
# for Kids 2

## More Little Bits of Wisdom for Little People

Honor Books

Tulsa, Oklahoma

*God's Little Instruction Book for Kids 2*
ISBN 1-56292-502-4
Copyright © 1998 by Honor Books, Inc.
P.O. Box 55388
Tulsa, Oklahoma 74155

Manuscript compiled by W. B. Freeman Concepts, Inc., Tulsa, Oklahoma

Illustrations by Julie Sawyer

# References

Unless otherwise indicated, all scriptures are taken from the *Holy Bible, New International Version®*. (NIV)® Copyright © 1973, 1978, 1984 by the International Bible Society. Used by permission of Zondervan Publishing House. All rights reserved.

Scripture quotations marked (ICB) are taken from the *International Children's Bible, New Century Version*, copyright © 1986, 1988 by Word Publishing, Dallas, Texas 75234. Used by permission.

Verses marked (TLB) are taken from *The Living Bible* Copyright © 1971. Used by permission of Tyndale House Publishers, Inc., Wheaton, Illinois 60189. All rights reserved.

Scripture quotations marked (NKJV) are taken from *The New King James Version*. Copyright © 1979, 1980, 1982, Thomas Nelson, Inc.

Scripture marked (GNB) is from the Good News Bible, Today's English Version, copyright © American Bible Society 1966, 1971, 1976. Used by permission.

All Scripture quotations marked KJV are taken from the *King James Version* of the Bible.

Scripture quotations marked CEV are taken from *The Contemporary English Version*, copyright © 1995 by the American Bible Society. All rights reserved.

# A Note to Parents

If you were one of the nearly half-million parents who enjoyed *God's Little Instruction Book for Kids*, you're going to love what we've done in *God's Little Instruction Book for Kids 2*. We're pleased to present more inspiration for you and your child, coupled with fun and cuddly illustrations to match. As with the first volume, this book is designed for children and includes quotes, rhymes and bits of wisdom for them to remember and cherish. Every quote has a Scripture verse to show the true meaning of the principle.

Read the quote and Scripture to your child, and ask them to tell you what it means in their own words. If they are unsure, explain it to them as you begin to show them how they can find directions they need for everything in life from God's Word.

If you find yourself reading *God's Little Instruction Book for Kids 2* after your kids have gone to bed, then we have done our job! This book, like the first, was meant for both the young, and the young at heart. Enjoy!

Sawyer

# Hands were made for helping.

A hard worker will get everything he wants.
— Proverbs 13:4 GNB

# You are one of God's best miracles!

Thank you for making me so
wonderfully complex!
It is amazing to think about.
Your workmanship is marvelous —
and how well I know it.
— Psalm 139:14 TLB

# See others as God sees them. See yourself as God sees you!

Do not think of anyone
as the world does. . . .
If anyone belongs to Christ,
then he is made new.
— 2 Corinthians 5:16-17 ICB

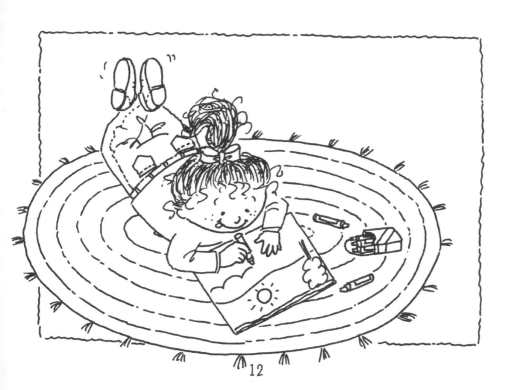

12

# Finish what you start.

Finishing is better than starting!
— Ecclesiastes 7:8 TLB

A quitter never wins.
A winner never quits!

I run straight for the
finish line.
— 1 Corinthians 9:26 GNB

Finish

14

# Of all the things you keep, keep your word.

God always keeps his word.
— Psalm 146:6 CEV

16

# God is always in the mood to hear a song from you.

Shout for joy to the LORD, all the earth,
burst into jubilant song with music.
— Psalm 98:4 NIV

# Need cheering up? Cheer up somebody else!

Kind words bring life.
— Proverbs 15:4 GNB

# Whatever you choose to be, choose to be good in God's eyes.

Do your best to be pure and faultless in God's sight and to be at peace with him.
— 2 Peter 3:14 GNB

Always tell the truth. That way you don't have to remember what you've said!

Lies will get any man into trouble, but honesty is its own defense.
— Proverbs 12:13 TLB

# A real friend always tells the truth.

An honest answer is a sign of true friendship.
— Proverbs 24:26 GNB

24

Give with
a smile!

God loves a cheerful giver.
— 2 Corinthians 9:7 NKJV

The best chance
to take is the chance
to do something nice
for another person.

Use every chance you have for
doing good.
— Ephesians 5:16 ICB

# It's never too late to forgive.

Forgive, and you
will be forgiven.
— Luke 6:37 NKJV

30

# Avoid following the crowd. Be an engine — not a caboose.

The LORD will make you the head and not the tail.
— Deuteronomy 28:13 NKJV

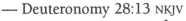

This gift doesn't cost anything,
doesn't make noise,
and doesn't need batteries.
One size fits all. Ideal for all ages.
And it can always be returned.
What is it?

A HUG!

Love each other with brotherly affection.
— Romans 12:10 TLB

33

# Please don't get too upset with me. I'm still under construction!

Man looks at the outward appearance,
but the LORD looks at the heart.
— 1 Samuel 16:7

You don't have to wait until you grow up to be a missionary. Tell someone about Jesus today!

Don't let anyone look down on you because
you are young, but set an example for the believers
in speech, in life, in love, in faith and in purity.
— 1 Timothy 4:12

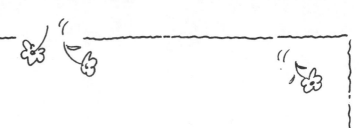

A thankful heart
is a happy heart.

In everything give thanks.
— 1 Thessalonians 5:18 NKJV

# Recipe for a good life: Just add Jesus.

Depend on the LORD. Trust
him, and he will take care
of you.
— Psalm 37:5 ICB

# What's the "good" word? God's Word — the Bible!

Your word is like a lamp for my feet
and a light for my way.
— Psalm 119:105 ICB

# Jesus gives you joy,
## joy,
### joy,
#### joy,
## down in your heart!

Yet I will rejoice in the LORD,
I will be joyful in God my Savior.
— Habakkuk 3:18

# Smile first.

Smiling faces make you happy, and
good news makes you feel better.
— Proverbs 15:30 GNB

# You don't need matches to be on fire for God!

Do not be lazy but work hard.
Serve the Lord with all your heart.
— Romans 12:11 ICB

# When you listen, you learn.

My child, listen to your father's teaching.
And do not forget your mother's advice.
— Proverbs 1:8 ICB

"Good boy!"

PUPPY

When God forgives you, it's like giving your soul a good bubble bath.

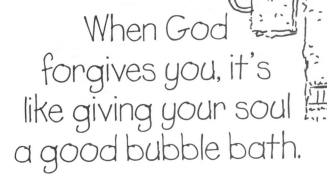

Wash away all my guilt and make me clean again.
— Psalm 51:2 ICB

# There's no place like home.

For we know that when this tent we live in now is
taken down . . . we will have wonderful
new bodies in heaven, homes that
will be ours forevermore.
— 2 Corinthians 5:1 TLB

52

# JOY is found in putting
## Jesus first.
## Others second.
## Yourself last.

This is what God commands:
that we believe in his Son, Jesus Christ,
and that we love each other.
— 1 John 3:23 ICB

JOY · JOY · JOY · JOY

# When Jesus knocks on the door of your heart – LET HIM IN!

Look! I have been standing at the door …
knocking. If anyone … opens the door,
I will come in and fellowship with him
and he with me.
— Revelation 3:20 TLB

# God never gets tired of your asking Him questions.

After three days [Joseph and Mary] found him.
Jesus was sitting in the Temple with the religious
teachers, listening to them and asking them questions.
— Luke 2:46 ICB

# Children are some of Jesus' favorite friends!

Let the little children come to me, and do not hinder them, for the kingdom of God belongs to such as these.
— Mark 10:14

I love you, Jesus!

Learn to smile
EVEN when there's
a hole in your umbrella!

He calms the storm . . .
— Psalm 107:29 NKJV

# Tomorrow is a brand-new blank page. Draw something beautiful on it!

I will give you a new heart
and put a new spirit in you.
— Ezekiel 36:26

# Love is the glue that holds families together.

You should be like one big happy family, full of sympathy toward each other, loving one another with tender hearts and humble minds.

— 1 Peter 3:8 TLB

63

A good time to say
"I love you" to someone you
care about is – ANY time!

All people will know that you are
my followers if you love each other.
— John 13:35 ICB

You can always share your secrets with God in prayer. He knows how to keep a secret forever.

He knows the secrets of every heart.
— Psalm 44:21 TLB

# Even little people can do big things.

I can do all things through Christ
because he gives me strength.
— Philippians 4:13 ICB

Make the person
you see in the mirror
each morning one of
your best buddies.

For in the image of God has God made man.
— Genesis 9:6

# Be a good worker.

The work of his hands rewards him.
— Proverbs 12:14

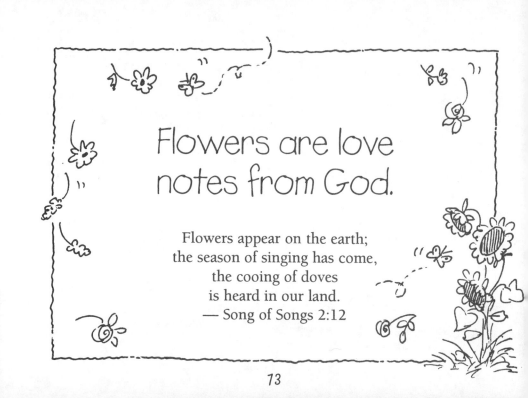

# Flowers are love notes from God.

Flowers appear on the earth;
the season of singing has come,
the cooing of doves
is heard in our land.
— Song of Songs 2:12

Doing something nice for someone is like giving him a cup of hot cocoa on a cold winter's day.

Being kind to the poor is like lending to the LORD. The LORD will reward you for what you have done.
— Proverbs 19:17 ICB

74

Everybody ought to know,
Everybody ought to know,
Everybody ought to know
Who Jesus is!

"Who do you say I am?"
Peter answered, "You are the Christ."
— Mark 8:29

The best thing
to do to someone
who hurts you is to do
a nice thing for them!

Love your enemies.
Do good to those who hate you.
— Luke 6:27 TLB

# If you don't keep your chin up, you can't see where you are going!

I have told you these things,
so that in me you may have peace.
In this world you will have trouble.
But take heart! I have overcome the world.
—John 16:33

Learning how to lose is
the first step to
becoming a good winner.

And let us run with perseverance
the race marked out for us.
— Hebrews 12:1

# God uses your hands to do His work.

For we are partners working
together for God.
— 1 Corinthians 3:9 GNB

# Jesus gives a happy heart!

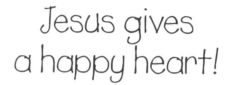

I will be glad and rejoice in You;
I will sing praise to Your name,
O Most High.
— Psalm 9:2 NKJV

# Every person has a Jesus-shaped hole in his heart.

My soul yearns for you in the night;
in the morning my spirit longs for you.
— Isaiah 26:9

# Never, never, NEVER give up on a friend.

A friend loves at all times,
and a brother is born for adversity.
— Proverbs 17:17

# Loving Grandmas and Grandpas are two of God's best gifts!

For by me your days will
be multiplied, And years of life
will be added to you.
— Proverbs 9:11 NKJV

# If you want to know a lot about a person, take a look at his friends.

He that walketh with wise men shall be wise:
but a companion of fools shall be destroyed.
— Proverbs 13:20 KJV

the Mustard See

# Even a little faith can result in a big miracle.

If you had faith even as small as a tiny mustard seed you could say to this mountain, 'Move!' and it would go far away.
— Matthew 17:20 TLB

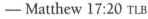

When nobody is around to hold your hand, remember that God is holding you in His hand.

My hand will sustain him;
surely my arm will
strengthen him.
— Psalm 89:21

94

When you want to do what God wants you to do, He will help you do it! Ask Him!

I am your God. I will make you strong
and will help you.
— Isaiah 41:10 ICB

96

# Be a good loser.
# Congratulate
# the winner.

Love is patient, love is kind. It does not envy,
it does not boast, it is not proud.
— 1 Corinthians 13:4

# Weeds can't grow in places where you have planted flowers.

Do not be overcome by evil,
but overcome evil with good.
— Romans 12:21

# When you help someone else, you help yourself.

He who refreshes others will himself be refreshed.
— Proverbs 11:25

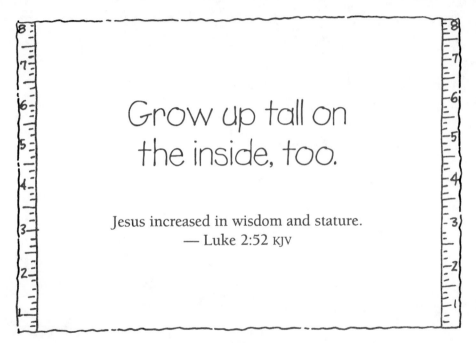

Grow up tall on
the inside, too.

Jesus increased in wisdom and stature.
— Luke 2:52 KJV

# It's nice to be important, but it's more important to be nice.

The greatest of these is love.
— 1 Corinthians 13:13 NKJV

When you have a fight,
the first one who says,
"I'm sorry, forgive me,"
is the winner.

When you are praying, first forgive
anyone you are holding a grudge against,
so that your Father in heaven will
forgive you your sins too.
— Mark 11:25 TLB

# You are never too young for God to use you.

Joash was seven years old
when he became king.
— 2 Kings 11:21 TLB

# Little people can still have big hearts.

Seek first the kingdom of God and His righteousness, and all these things shall be added to you.
— Matthew 6:33 NKJV

Additional copies of this book and other titles in the God's Little
Instruction Book series are available at your local bookstore.

*God's Little Instruction Book*
*God's Little Instruction Book for Women*
*God's Little Instruction Book for Men*
*God's Little Instruction Book for Dad*
*God's Little Instruction Book for Mom*
*God's Little Instruction Book for Kids*
*God's Little Instruction Book on Love*
*God's Little Instruction Book on Character*
*God's Little Instruction Book on Success*
*God's Little Instruction Book on Prayer*

Honor Books
Tulsa, Oklahoma